ame

rica, MI

Sasha Banks
NE
POEMS

co·im·press

normal, illinois

Copyright © 2020 by Sasha Banks

Published by co•im•press
Normal, Illinois
www.coimpress.com
co•im•press is a recognized 501(c)(3) nonprofit literary organization.

Printed in the USA by Bookmobile

Distributed to the trade by Small Press Distribution
1341 Seventh Street, Berkeley, CA 94710
www.spdbooks.org

Cover and Book Design by co•im•press
Cover Art by Michael McCluskey
Production Assistant: Gabrielle Brown
Editorial Assistant: Katelyn Kern

First Edition 2020

ISBN: 978-1-947918-04-7

Contents

Recollect • *1*
uhmareka, *pre-collapse*: one • *3*
Blood Moon • *4*
Portrait of My Sister's Ankle Tied in Ribbon • *5*
Capitol Suite • *7*
Sasha Fells the Wildwood • *11*
Oh, the Soil Recites • *13*
And When It Doesn't Happen • *14*
Upon Visiting Harriet Tubman's Grave • *16*
uhmareka, *collapse*: two • *17*
Of Steam • *18*
Sasha at Monticello • *19*
uhmareka, *post collapse*: three • *20*
Upon Visiting Harriet Tubman's Grave Pt. 2 • *21*
Upon Visiting Harriet Tubman's Grave Pt. 3 • *22*
If I Say I Hate My Country • *23*
Ahistorical: the Founder's Farce • *25*
Sasha's Blade on Mount Rushmore • *27*
From Canfield Green Apartments, Tituba, Rekia, and Cynthia Watch Michael Fall • *28*
Presidential Order • *31*
america, MINE • *59*
uhmareka, *post post collapse*: four • *60*
Ritual, ritual • *62*
Gone Suite • *64*
Blessed It Was • *67*
Untitled (But Still a Warning, Though) • *68*
God Bless america • *69*

To Remember Now • **70**
Uhmarekin History Suite • **71**
Sasha's Waltz on the Wreckage • **77**

Acknowledgments • **81**

> ... there's nobody gonna sleep here tonight!
> Nobody's gonna sleep here, honey ... nobody.
> ... NOBODY.
> —Nina Simone

> ... every now and then I think you might
> like to hear something from us nice
> and easy, but ... we never ever do nothing
> nice and easy. We always do it nice
> and rough.
> —Tina Turner

Recollect

Draw a map of america from memory—don't include the state lines

Draw a picture of Abraham Lincoln from memory.

Draw a map of america from memory—place a star in the general area of the nation's capitol.

Tell the story of how George Washington chopped down the cherry tree—if you don't know, make it up.

Who was Robert E. Lee?

Draw a picture of the White House from memory.

Where was the last place you saw the old flag?

What was the old flag made out of?

Write the Gettysburg Address—if you don't know it, make it up.

Write the pledge of allegiance—if you don't know it, make it up.

What is the new flag made out of?

What was Ronald Reagan's favorite color?

Please name all 56 signees of the Declaration of Independence—if you don't know them, make them up.

Who was the 45th president of america?

What shade of white is the White House:

a) Egg Shell b) Supreme c) The Driven Snow d) The Great White e) Whiter Than White

Draw Thomas Jefferson's family tree.

Did someone/something live in the Washington Monument? If so, who/what?

Draw a map of america from memory—include the state lines.

What did the end of america sound like? Did you dance? Why? Why not?

Do you believe in ghosts (essentially, do you believe in ancestors)?

What do you miss that left with america?

Draw a map of america from memory—include the Trail of Tears.

Draw a map of america from memory—place a star in the general area where police murdered a Black person.

Does July 4, 1776 have any significance to you? Explain.

Finish this line: Oh I _____ I was in the Land of Cotton.

Finish this line: Glory, glory _____.

Draw a map of america—include the ports of the Trans-Atlantic Slave Trade.

What is a curse?

Draw a map of america from memory—place a star to indicate sites of Japanese Internment Camps.

How did the 45th president of america die?

Can land be cursed? If so, can a curse be broken off of the land?

Draw a map of Uhmareka.

uhmareka, *pre collapse*: one

a blonde braid is unraveling
a glass of milk is spilt
a blue eye is gouged
an alphabet is cursed
a border is crumbling
a nose is broken
a backbone is curving
a redline is smudged
a dollar is ripping
a badge is rusted
a train track is rotting
a gate is leaning

Blood Moon

The first
screams wedged out from
between the soil's teeth
hung like a handsome clergy of
sorrows.

It was
a season of
death; the stench of hope and
knowing was old and upsetting
the blood.

All this
history is
a howling plague under
a blood moon, strung up brilliantly
inside

of this
american
sky. On the radio,
voices are a horror of fists.
Silence,

it breaks:
"Not guilty." The
heat that summer was its
own song: a long, impossible
justice.

Portrait of My Sister's Ankle Tied in Ribbon

for Ariana

We inherit the sky
somehow. You and I
have circled the alchemy
of blood and magic,
time and ancestors,
anchors and flesh,
but I have no good
answer for how to live
on the ground, Ariana, not
as long as
my own body is a wounded kite
convulsing in the wind of history;
not as long as leaving my body
is the only way I know
to outlive it. When our people
collapsed to small ruins, we
watched our own black feet
begin to lift off the ground: black
balloon bodies versed in
ascension or survival, which might
be the same thing. If my love
could be the ribbon
that my age has woven
up to this moment,
I would tie it 'round your ankle
as you began to float above my head,
keep you inside your body—tethered
to this earth. Sister,

what spectacular weight
is blackness like this that
belittles all the sciences with
its burden and weightlessness?
To reconcile a heaven
into this earth, these
bodies, is an ancient dance done
between cloud and soil,
despite the gravity, despite
the gravity.

Capitol Suite

Negromania

King Kong climbs the
washington monument
&
the seat of the lincoln
memorial is empty &
the reflection pool
is grim with crows
& the laughter
of two ghosts[i] haunts
jefferson's memorial
as they swallow
nickels into
their veiled throats
&
Fannie[ii] tramples down
Pennsylvania avenue,
stopping to pull
the capitol's steeple
from her giant's foot,
a long shadow
over Aunt Jemima
and Mammy sunbathing
on the white house
lawn,
&
Jemima winks

at Jesse[iii] painting
a picket fence
with the blood of
Jesus &
the Sphinx has pissed
on a rug in the oval
office &
Aiyana[iv] is twirling on
the roof
of the pentagon, shooting
seeds from her mouth
until she spins
in a grove of watermelons
&&
&
God parts
her hair down
the middle,
greasing her scalp
on the supreme
court steps.

---

i. Betty Hemings was enslaved, in Virginia in 1761, to John Wales who fathered six of her children; his daughter Martha, and her husband Thomas Jefferson, inherited Betty and her children including her daughter, Sally Hemings, who had six children fathered by Thomas Jefferson.

ii. Fannie Lou Hamer was a Civil Rights leader and activist who addressed Mississippi's Democratic Convention Committee, in 1964, with a speech on the violent resistance she encountered in her effort to register to vote. Her speech garnered great attention and press coverage, which was interrupted and redirected, at the request of Lyndon B. Johnson.

iii. Jesse Washington was seventeen years old when he was tried and convicted for murder in Waco, TX in 1916. He was sentenced to death and immediately lynched over a bonfire in front of City Hall. His remains were collected as souvenirs and photographs of his lynching were printed and sold as postcards.

iv. Aiyana Stanley Jones was a seven-year-old girl shot and killed by officer Joseph Weekley, during a raid in Detroit, MI, in 2010; he was cleared of all charges.

Negromancy

God shouts
at a kink snagged
on her
comb &
Aiyana sings,
*Black
cat cross
my path, think
every day's gonna
be my last.
Lord, have mercy
on this land
of mine: we
all gonna get it,
in due time.*[i]
& the Sphinx recites
the gettysburg address
& Jesse asks
for a cup of water &
Mammy leans in,
says to Jemima,
"that mouse, gonna
swallow the housecat."
& Fannie howls
when she finds an earth
stuck to a piece

of hard candy, in her
front pocket &
two ghosts are heard
calling out
the names of
the young and dead
&
the crows confess
that they have teeth
& lincoln's seat is
still empty &
King Kong
whispers the name
his mother calls him.

---

i Excerpt from Nina Simone's "Mississippi Goddamn"

Sasha Fells the Wildwood

i.
Mhm. The poplars know
how to hold death. Keep it
still. But I'm swinging the axe.
They're all around the city:
eyeless and staring
even to the dirt under
my nails. Peopling the
bayous. Hungry. Look.

ii.
Last night was that dream
again: me and Jesus
pulling nails out of our feet
at the lip of the Mississippi
Delta. Somewhere, Coretta
is calling for Martin
to come down from a sycamore.
He's just a boy, here, but
he weeps and the sky
is ripped at the belly.

iii.
They shifted shapes. But I know.
The rocking chair, the banister,
nightstand, porch steps, vanity. I know,
and I am swinging the axe.

iv.
Don't laugh. I couldn't have been
the only black child
who didn't trust the forest; who saw it,
from her dark window, turning itself
into rows of small coffins. A silence
like that—all the time smirking
with no mouth. Knew my terror
and loved it.

v.
Watch *me*, now.
I'm swinging this axe.
I come back for all of this summer
and give my flesh to it,
undressed in its hot breath.
Watch. Just steady on
this axe I'm swingin'. I run
through this klan of cypresses
whirling their lassos above
their branches. They want
to make me their strangest fruit.
But look.
How the axe humbles the wood
to a stacked history
of its noosed unions to this skin.
A clean cut. And now,
so much firewood.

Oh, the Soil Recites

The soil forgets
nothing.
Everything becomes
a record. And oh,
the soil recites:
the name, each
blood that scattered
when his body
hit the earth
like
a rescinded
prayer.
The soil
recites
the million
blades of grass
that leaned to
the east
and became a palm;
how it held him.
How it holds
him in this long,
dirty slumber.

And When It Doesn't Happen

there is a tenderness afforded,
when my father asks me
why the officer didn't
kill him,
that afternoon
in east Texas
when he was a black crow
perched on the freeway's shoulder.
My explanations
falling apart on my fingertips
like an offering of embers.
In this moment
suspended on the axis of my storied blood,
every minute that wore the same
face when it saw my ancestors to their
knees stops blinking, is
already laughing
at my stupid breath
collecting itself to say,
"I don't know why you aren't
dead by now, Dad. I don't know why
you aren't a breath shucked from
the black slick husk of your body,
by now."
We haunt the air in gathered silence,
my father and I, startled by ourselves,
our confusion at his blood out
of sight and in his body.

He was still a whole man and
we did not know
how to celebrate that.

Upon Visiting Harriet Tubman's Grave

I dressed my hair
in white flowers
to make myself
beautiful for her,
because she could
be anywhere
watching another
of her liquid daughters
come to dissolve
over her mouth and
say her name without
saying it at all. She
knew everything
there is to weep about,
will be to weep
about, was to weep
about. And there
she was, a temple six
feet under my shoes
and the long winter.

uhmareka, *collapse*: two

I saw a city crumbling into the mouth of
a many-headed beast. The beast was not
the terror, she was my cousin; the terror
was the sudden knowing that all
empires are made of paper and
damned religions.

I will tell you the horror,
and that is of the crumbling city's silence.
Yes, its people had mouths. And yes,
they were stuffed with the broke-off limbs
of the conquered, refusing their shouting breath.
Elbow, elbow, fibula, knee: the innocuous
become the silencer, the way the small
do become the mighty with new
big bodies and opposable tongues.

Everything does weep, but oh
how it growls, when the wailing is done.
If anger, on the other side of fear,
is rage, this city was delivered to
death, with savage conviction.

I saw the beast lick the sinew
from her jaws, and the city—it was
still and clean, new and clean, bright
and clean and clean and clean as
the blood on my face.

Of Steam

A black boy burned the lake; with his hot hands, he did.
Some boys are so full of their own heat.
And how's a city surrounded by trees gonna keep a boy like that?
But the world is made of so much water, and none of it holy enough.

Some boys are so full of their own heat.
A black body will dance when it knows where to put the brimstone.
But the world is made of so much water, and none of it holy enough.
Every sidewalk is bloody with superstition.

A black body will dance when it knows where to put the brimstone.
Its breath and smoke promenade like all warring benedictions.
Every sidewalk is bloody with superstition.
The pavement is thirsty for something to call blessed.

Breath and smoke promenade like warring benedictions.
Death is the body that can be robbed of its blood on any street corner,
when the pavement is thirsty for something to call blessed, when saints
are burning on the south side, and their cities are drinking their sweat.

Sasha at Monticello

I inhale the ghosts and find
the sweat, ancient and heavy.
I am inhaling the ghosts and here
is the fear, crusted and broke. I
am inhaling the ghosts and
there is the hair, matted and furious.
I am inhaling the ghosts and there
is the blood, hot and sparkling.
Here is the mouth, soft and
splintered. Here are the hands,
taking (everything).
There are the eyes, glossed and
troubled. There is the whip, dead
and done. I am the ghosts I have
inhaled, and this is the house
blown down, blown to corpse,
blown to bones, blown to dust,
to nothing at all.

uhmareka, *post collapse*: three

You will remember nothing but the taste of salt and how it's in everything, and how it never changes even though everything else does, and so you will cry and cry and be fed.

A woman will stand in the street and open her mouth, one summer night. Noiseless for hours until she retches up a star, hot thing covered in mucus.

I want to say something like *it turns out that the sun had a face, which implies a mouth that knew all your names,* but the truth is there will never have been any sun; only the North star, after all. It will fall down and land behind a woman's house, in Detroit. It will be dark for weeks, and everyone's eyes will glow.

Here and now will be the faded kind of memory like waking from a dream that loosens its grip as you become wider and wider awake. At the grocery store, you will hear someone whistling the old anthem. They will not be able to remember more than "oh say can you…?" Nobody will. Such is the case with ruins, ancient histories, blurry faces everywhere smeared by the fists of their conquerors.

Before today ends, statues will be plucked from their high places all over the country; this should be the first sign, but white people will not see themselves in this sure demise. They will learn.

There will be no flag, anymore.

Many will dream of eagles eaten by crows; pecked to death by crows. A woman will tell of seeing a crow pulling all the feathers from a dead eagle. None will remember this time, but the crows will. And so they will eat the grudge for your sakes.

america will be done and you will know it when the statue of liberty sits down to wash her face in the Hudson; her skin will be black. Your grandmothers will weep.

Upon Visiting Harriet Tubman's Grave Pt. 2

I wanted to ask her
how to make a
warning of your blood
to paint the threshold
of your enemy; how
to bite off the head
of hatred; how to
love a country
that hated you, first.
But
I dug and dug
at the soil until
I thought
I was touching her
face; until I thought
she was doing
the same.

Upon Visiting Harriet Tubman's Grave Pt. 3

My kin
took my face in
her palm's muddy bone
and the orbs of
her vanished eyes
were small
valleys of violet
that blurred bodies
ran through, crude
as wind. ten thousand
crows dove
into the crooked
river of her mouth,
now a split bone
in the skull.
their myriad screams
became her voice,
a twisted line
of sound that said,
"shake off this ancient
sorrow, kindred. my back
is broken for you."

If I Say I Hate My Country

It could come back
like a chorus or
a bitch of cancer.

Tumor, attack
of the heart, pebble
in the bloodstream,
carousel of
spinning vertebrae,
sunk kidney, strayed
faculties.

I heard the pastor
say *unforgiveness
manifests in the
liver.* Or
*unforgiveness is
a ghost that haunts
the intestine
and wears the
liver, loose, like
a new face.*
Or *unforgiveness
creeps among the
innards, slipping
noiselessly by
the blind organs to
seize the liver.*

All this, longhand
meaning, "either your
country will kill
you or your
hatred will."

And what lucky paradox
is this body, killing
itself in defense
of itself. Allowed
to own nothing

not even the malice
of its own
black heart.

Ahistorical: The Founders' Farce

Once upon a time, Christopher Columbus sneezed and the constellations were formed as George Washington stood below them and chopped down a cherry tree to build the Arc. The rain came and bled on everything; swallowed Robert E. Lee and spit him out onto the shore where the Wright brothers spotted him from their hot-air balloon just before crashing into the thick of Yellowstone Park. The commotion startled Lewis, who ran to find Clark (who was, at that moment, building a log cabin) and the quake was so great, it shook the land into fifty pieces and the states got their shapes when, suddenly, a thread of lightning slid across the sky, striking Benjamin Franklin right between the eyes and from that day on, all his dreams were premonitions: one night he dreamt of iron stitches holding the West together and in the morning, the railroad was sewn across the Mississippi River, into which, John Rockefeller had just tossed his third penny when the Spirit of St. Louis came floating up from below the current saying, "Fee-fi-fo-fum! Of all your wishes, I may grant one." Rockefeller cried, "I wish my hands were made of money!" and in a blink, his palms turned to bills, and his fingers, coins. He buried them into the soil and a plume of oil shot from the ground, ruining Betsy Ross's best dress. She quickly began a new skirt, stitching a pattern so beautiful she hung it in her window for all to admire, including her neighbor, John Wilkes Booth, who waited for nightfall to thieve the skirt from her window where Abraham Lincoln, out walking his cocker spaniel, stood mere feet away watching the skirt be carried off; he confronted Booth, saying if it weren't returned by midnight, he would announce to everyone what Booth had done the following week, at the town hall meeting, wherein the country would finally be named, but Booth refused. Days later, John Hancock stood before the town and drew the country's name from a hat of suggestions written on slips of paper. In his hand was the inscription "marigold," but on account of his failing eyesight and the author's scribbled cursive, he misread it, "america" and as the town applauded, Abraham rose to his feet and began "Four days and seven hours ago, our neighbor, John Wilkes…" when just then, Booth leapt out from behind the shadows and fired a fatal bullet into Abraham's chest. Booth was swiftly apprehended and at his funeral, Abraham's casket was draped with Betsy's stolen skirt, which the townspeople declared the official American Rag.

Sasha's Blade on Mount Rushmore

I straddle the last face and erupt the screech of steel, stone. The motion repeated back and forth against the granite's glory until it is a dumb rock. "It's over, honey." I, patting George's clenched jaw. I come down from the mountainside and look upon this new ruin; below me, a wicked pile of noses at my feet like flowers.

From Canfield Green Apartments, Tituba, Rekia, And Cynthia Watch Michael Fall

Street: In apartment wall. Across the street. Hot August. He/Michael[1] running away. From off'cer {& silver arrow}. Th' sound. One/two, three; fffourrrr. Five sixsevennnn (ate?) I/T/Tituba[2] cursing in wall. Moaning 'cause I've sawn it before and before again. & crying –AGAIN THIS. OH, - HE HANDS UP I/T/ME/TITUBA SAWED THEY THERE ON THE SKY UP. Speaked with some shout and I/Tituba, just in a walls now nothing no body just gone. No one hears me because dead means still silent hushed as a blown candle. Him/he/Michael bloods and bloods on the street for hour then hour hour & hour. But I saw when he go into the up and his face looked just still still and boy. I/Tituba want to tell Him/M –COME STAY THIS WITH ME. WON TOOTH THREE FOUREVER, MICHAEL. MICHAEL? MICHAEL!

---

1 Michael Brown, 18—a boy fatally shot by Ferguson police officer Darren Wilson in August 2014.

2 Tituba—a Barbadian woman enslaved in Danvers, MA, was the first to be accused of witchcraft during the Salem Witch Trials of the seventeenth century.

Street: In the window. August, now. Michael he walk walking from this thissswh-te m-n. Michael a silver behind you MichaelMichaelMMMichael look around you back behind. Both sky palms. Both. One pop {had a great fall}. Cynthia shaking on a wire & Tituba (in) the wall mad as fire. She hot piss pisssvinegar. Rekia[3] (my nnname ago) in the window I, –AGAIN THIS? OH, HIS HANDS UP! Rekia (mine name) watch'd his head catch'd a wh-te m-n's silver. Cynthia shooking everything. Michael? You see Rekia (a name then) look look look the window, Michael! {so red so red the street on, clock spin spin spin spin I know four. Times.} Every wh-te m-n a bird flyed from guilt away? oh me. sour ghost girl husk me Rekia gone in window. Michael go into some up where. I see I ssssawhim go. & his face a beam sweet {it comes off I tttthink. Michael's face. a new one just on after this now time. and hair too. teeth? a lights sunlike a stars on waters I tttthink. I see I ssssaw that. Too}. Say Rekia (mmme) –MICHAEL? WHERE ARE YOU?

---

[3] Rekia Boyd, 22—a woman fatally shot by off-duty Chicago police detective, Dante Servin in March 2012.

Street: Telephone wire. Nine Augusts. BOOM {s i x them}. Mike runnnnn BOOM he crumbs. {crumbs?} C RRR U MMM B LLLLL E. He did. Was a man. There was a man put six ssssilver missile in Mike. & Rekia she –AGAIN THIS? OH, HIM HANDS UP! Tituba and –I SAW THEM THERE ON THE SKY UP. Palm there. Palm too over tttthere. Now. Mike d o w n. Mike. Cynthiiiiiia[4] me. Your eyes is there over. Mouth a car under. You red-ing the street long on four. YYYou falling still? Look. Up me. Here, Mike. See? He lay. He down done. Dead don't wwwwalk but we move. {& no names, no name after here this. Some dead? name only living on a mouth in a teeths a tongue}. Dead don't walk. BOOM, like that. Just down just coming we when a blood calling. A dying kin's name is our name. & we answer {to}, it. Come Mike away up. Walls cal'mity. {calamity?} C O LLLL A PP SSSS E. Uh, b o d y you? {Smoke?} Dust. You body got fall'd. Went deaded down dropped you did but. You every skins all come new, now here up. Look'd. & Mike. Telephone wire {gasp} he shhhh by. He go. Go{ne}? Palms for Mike. Hair & a teeth some shine. I says, —MIKE! CAN YOU HEAR THEM REMEMBERING?

---

[4] Cynthia Wesley, 14—a girl killed in a terror attack on the 16th Street Baptist Church of Birmingham, AL, when the United Klans of America detonated a bomb in September 1963.

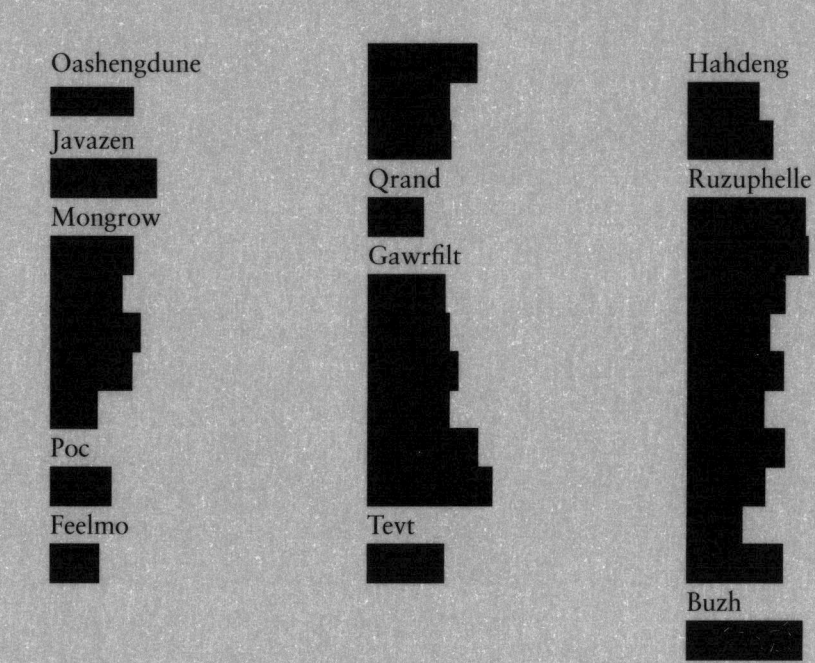

Prissodenshull Urder

Oashengdune

Javazen

Mongrow

Poc

Feelmo

Qrand

Gawrfilt

Tevt

Hahdeng

Ruzuphelle

Buzh

Prissodenshull Urder

Hadkeng

Ruzuphelle

Buzh

Grand

Gawfilt

Tevr

Oashengdune

Javzen

Mongrow

Poc

Feelmo

Prizodintyool Utter

Wurshita

Shefison

Chagzin

Fambjorn

Poag

Fihmur

Pez

Lunqan

Daft

Nissan

Booch

Booch

Prizodintyool Utter

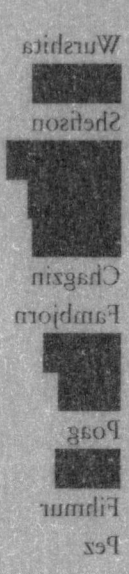

Nissan	Lungan	Wurshita
Booch		Sheltson
Booch	Daft	Chaggin
		Fambjorn
		Poag
		Fibmur
		Pez

Prizedenjal Orter

Boocana
Lenke

Hizs

Coolish
Hewfa
Rowseffe

Makill

Fumo
Piss

Wullseh

Obah

Prizedenjal Orter

[redacted]
Fumo
Piss

Boocana
Lenke
[redacted]
Hizs
[redacted]
Makill
[redacted]
Wullsch

[redacted]
Coolish
Hewia
Rowseffe
[redacted]
Obah

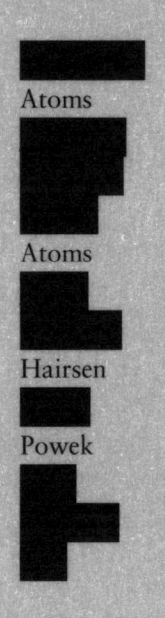

Presitenchull Orhtar

Atoms

Atoms

Hairsen

Powek

Beukanna

Crandt
Hezz

Cliiflan

Vissin

Culush

Rosifeld

Codder

Colindin

Presitenchull Orhtar

Culush	Beukanna	Aroms
Rosfield	Crandt	Aroms
	Heza	Hairsen
	Cliifan	Powek
Codder		
Colndin	Vissin	

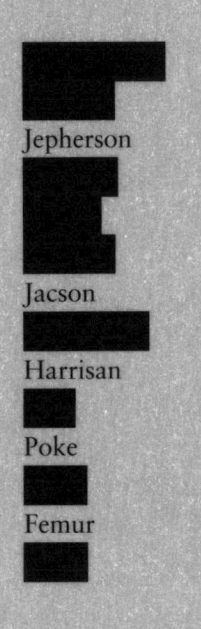

Presadential Order

Jepherson

Jacson

Harrisan

Poke

Femur

Haze

Whover

Trueman

Carder

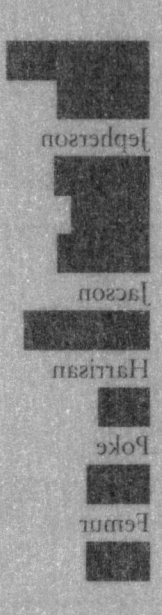

Presadential Order

Whover

Trueman

Carder

Haxe

Jepherson

Jacson

Harrisan

Poke

Femur

Presidential Order

Washington	Buchanan	Harding
Adams	Lincoln	Coolidge
Jefferson	Johnson	Hoover
Madison	Grant	Roosevelt
Monroe	Hayes	Truman
Adams	Garfield	Eisenhower
Jackson	Arthur	Kennedy
Van Buren	Cleveland	Johnson
Harrison	Harrison	Nixon
Tyler	Cleveland	Ford
Polk	McKinley	Carter
Taylor	Roosevelt	Reagan
Fillmore	Taft	Bush
Pierce	Wilson	Clinton
		Bush
		Obama

Presidential Order

Washington	Buchanan	Harding
Adams	Lincoln	Coolidge
Jefferson	Johnson	Hoover
Madison	Grant	Roosevelt
Monroe	Hayes	Truman
Adams	Garfield	Eisenhower
Jackson	Arthur	Kennedy
Van Buren	Cleveland	Johnson
Harrison	Harrison	Nixon
Tyler	Cleveland	Ford
Polk	McKinley	Carter
Taylor	Roosevelt	Reagan
Fillmore	Taft	Bush
Pierce	Wilson	Clinton
		Bush
		Obama

President   Order

Wash	Buc a an	ng
Adams	Linco	Coolidge
Je son	Johnson	Hoover
Mad	Gr nt	Roos
Monroe	Hayes	uman
da	Garfield	Eisenhower
J on	thur	Ke edy
Van Buren	Cleveland	Johnson
Harr n	ris n	Nix
T ler	leveland	Ford
olk	Kin	C r
T ylor	Roosevelt	R ag
Fi lm e	Taft	h
Pier e	Wils	lint
		sh
		O

President Order

Wash	Buc an	ng
Adams	Linco	Coolidge
Je son	Johnson	Hoover
Mad	Gr nt	Roos
Monroe	Hayes	uman
da	Garfield	Eisenhower
J on	thur	Ke edy
Van Buren	Cleveland	Johnson
Harr n	ris n	Nix
T ler	leveland	Ford
olk	Kin	C r
T ylor	Roosevelt	R ag
Fillm e	Taft	h
Pier e	Wils	lint
		sh
		O

Preside   O   er

ash	Buchanan	Harding
ms	Lincoln	oo
so	ohn	over
dison	G nt	oo
Monroe	yes	Truman
Adams	Garfi	how
ack	Arthur	enne
Van ren	and	oh
Harrison	H on	x
Tyler	level	F d
o	McKinley	Carter
aylo	Ro velt	R ag
illmore	ft	u h
Pie	Wil on	n o
		Bush
		b ma

Preside O er

ash	Buchanan	Harding
ms	Lincoln	oo
so	ohn	over
dison	G nt	oo
Monroe	yes	Truman
Adams	Garfi	how
ack	Arthur	enne
Van ren	and	oh
Harrison	H on	x
Tyler	level	F d
o	McKinley	Carter
aylo	Ro velt	R ag
illmore	ft	u h
Pie	Wil on	n o
		Bush
		b ma

                        denti   de

         a   i   uc   an   din
         da   L   ol   ge
         ff   h   o   over
         Ma   G   se
          o o   s   m
           ams   el   Ei   n   o
           ck   t u   n   dy
          n   n   vel n   n
          a   rr   N   n
         T   r   v   or
          k   M K   C   t
          ylo   t   aga
          ll   Ta   B   h
         e ce   l o   t
                                                              us
                                                                m

Presidential Ord

Washington	Buchanan	Harding
Adams		Coolidge
Jefferson	Johnson	Hoover
Madison	Grant	Roosevelt
	Hayes	Truman
Adams	Garfield	Eisenhower
Jackson	Arthur	
Van Buren	Cleveland	Johnson
Harrison	Harrison	Nixon
Tyler		Ford
Polk		Carter
		Reagan
Fillmore	Taft	Bush
Pierce	Wilson	
		Bush

Presidential Ord

Washington	Buchanan	Harding
Adams		Coolidge
Jefferson	Johnson	Hoover
Madison	Grant	Roosevelt
	Hayes	Truman
Adams	Garfield	Eisenhower
Jackson	Arthur	
Van Buren	Cleveland	Johnson
Harrison	Harrison	Nixon
Tyler		Ford
Polk		Carter
		Reagan
Fillmore	Taft	Bush
Pierce	Wilson	
		Bush

side   Order

Washington	Buchanan	
Adams		Coolidge
Jefferson		
		Roosevelt
Monroe	Hayes	Truman
Adams	Garfield	
Jackson	Arthur	Kennedy
		Nixon
	Cleveland	Ford
	McKinley	Carter
	Roosevelt	
Fillmore		Bush
Pierce	Wilson	Clinton
		Bush

Side	Order		
Washington			
Adams			
Jefferson			
Monroe	Hayes	Truman	
Adams	Garfield		Roosevelt
Jackson	Arthur	Kennedy	Coolidge
		Nixon	
	Cleveland	Ford	
	McKinley	Carter	
	Roosevelt		
Fillmore	Wilson	Clinton	Bush
Pierce		Bush	

Pres   O

	Buchanan	Harding
	Lincoln	
		Hoover
	Grant	
		Truman
Jackson		Kennedy
Van Buren		Johnson
Harrison		Nixon
	Cleveland	
Polk		
Taylor	Roosevelt	
	Taft	
Pierce		

Pres   O

	Buchanan	Harding
	Lincoln	
		Hoover
	Grant	
		Truman
Jackson		Kennedy
Van Buren		Johnson
Harrison		Nixon
	Cleveland	
Polk		
Taylor	Roosevelt	
	Taft	
Pierce		

Presidentia

Adams   Coolidge

                          McKinley
Polk

                                       Clinton

Presidential

Adams

Coolidge

Polk

McKinley

Clinton

resident   Order

                                                        Obama

President Order

Obama

america, MINE

the spit upon this/country's flag is mine and/I do/not weep at it/consider the twisted shape of grief about/the mouth upon learning the beast/under the bed has always been your country/careful, citizen/this nation will name you/daughter/while its tongue/sucks the muscle from every dark body/you have loved to the edge of this/vanished second/I let the rage be/like water/this time/drinking and drinking until/my darkness marries/my eyes to blindness/and I am/led by the ghosts still/ awake/in the soil/still/thirsty from/below/the fear/is under my heel/now/there are multitudes/in my third rib and/we are not/asking anymore/do you see us now/this is the last kindness/we will have your sweat/and dress you in your own/curses/oh country/what I mean to say/is/all the living after/this/will be the vengeance.

uhmareka, *post post collapse*: four

endings exist, ripped curtains, shock

and chrome and clay and captives and coconut oil,
patriots are vanishing or
existing less and less, aftermath

magnolias exist, their misty breath exists, and
whatever bodies below them are held still,
still and always; light caught in a mirror is held,
a daughter's name held in a mouth, a daughter's
hand held at a crosswalk, crosswalks exist

808s exist, subwoofers, streets, sidewalks,
and saints, saints and sidewalks exist
pavement, parked cars, patrols vanishing or existing
less and less

water exists and thirst on the tongue, thirst exists;
and doors and demons and decisions exist too, danger exists;
hush-hush is vanishing, fences and maps vanishing too,
little men and their little militaries are vanishing or
existing less and less

you stand at the bathroom sink, brushing
your teeth in the mirror, when you notice
the reflection of some bygone era walk across
the floor of the hallway behind you, you turn around,
she shows you her hands, muddy,
vines under her nails, you face the mirror, and she is gone

hands exist, hands, hoodies, hymns, hind legs,
and haha; haha exists, victory and violins too
808s and dancing men, full as a magnolia
with the wind in its hair exist; it's joy and
that exists too, aftermath

living is loud, but not the way dying is loud;
on the ground some found magic, the sound of
prayers exists, round bellies of children exist,
children exist, aftermath;

there is your mother under a streetlight calling
your name after sunset and you answer, you answer;
answering exists, answering exists, which means
the living exist, existing exists, and maybe
so much death is vanishing or existing less and less.

Ritual, ritual

i.
    In kindergarten I said,
    "I pledge in legions
    to the flag…" in childish
    recitation. I learned
    to say "allegiance," and
    I learned the national
    anthem, and I learned
    to breathe despite the
    the necklace of tradition,
    'round my throat
    a string of knuckles.

ii.
    my country,
    tears of these sweet lands of liberty: of thee, I sing.
    land where my fathers died, land where the pilgrims lied from every mountainside.

    let freedom ring.

iii.
    and i learned.
    and i learned.
    and i learned.
    and i learned.
    and i learned.

iv.
   Every independence day,
   my niece believes
   the firecrackers outside
   are gunshots, and does not
   come outside all night.

Gone Suite

Poof
Then one day the world was so new,
the names of things fell as dead leaves
at our feet. *Other, Nigger, Urban,*
all seated in the order of their births, ate
the hair of their dead mother: a grief, umbilical.
And now someone runs faster, it seems,
without the weight of a name or its consequence.

Slight

September 2018 a man in Connecticut says his right arm is disappearing June 2019 a couple in Maine says their shadows have disappeared December 2019 24 cases of children ceasing to grow beyond their third birthdays are reported in New Hampshire April 2020 279 people are confirmed to have permanently lost their voices in Vermont October 2020 6 people in Iowa reportedly weigh 0lbs and 0oz despite displaying no changes in their physical appearance May 2021 12 people in Utah are investigated after their fingerprints were found to have disappeared January 2022 members of a small community in Wyoming begin to shrink February 2022 the search begins for 6 people blown away by a gust of wind in Montana November 2023 in Oregon a mother and her 2 sons are taken for medical and scientific study after their bodies become entirely transparent June 2024 video of a man on a beach in Massachusetts goes viral when he walks on the sand and leaves no footprints August 2024 a man in Idaho is uninjured after jumping from the 27th floor and landing, light as a feather.

The Only Ones Who See It Now
Are the Ones Who ~~Couldn't~~ *Wouldn't Then*
In this new quiet, I admit there was a time when I wanted to befriend It; stroke its face and tell It my name. I didn't see, didn't think to look at the dirt and continents, blood and languages, the names and people under its nails. Before I knew It wanted to kill me, I wanted It to smile at me. It is dead now: a ghost, meaning everything about It can be seen in the dark as It often is, these days in the Ancient Suburbs. A man says its mammoth body collapsed and came up through the floorboards. I say yes, because I remember. It skulks under another man's bed, he says It had hands the size of an 18-wheeler. I say yes, because I remember. A woman saw It pulling at the ill-fit skin of its face, and I say yes because I remember. *My God my heavens my goodness my lord* they say *but was It always so loud?* I say no. No. All the time I knew It, It was quiet as a blind eye.

Blessed It Was

It was the sound, a
herd of clouds dragging
their bellies, full and
scraping the sky. Every
lifted chin, every upturned
face saw it all come down: oil
and songs falling with
the weight of theft.
Arizona sunken below
80 feet of tongues. Every hip
in Florida wading through cubic
feet of hair. A man fixed a tongue
into his mouth and called
the names of his unknown
kin. Falling gold, falling children,
land, silk, innocence, and gods.
"Return, returned…" said
the tongues. Spines lengthened
with the whole truth, now.
Here was some spectacular
abundance. Blessed it was. And
blessed is the wealth that returns.

Untitled (But Still a Warning Though)

Yes, there will be blood;
it's how everything arrives.
The blood will not be ours, anymore.
Gnashing teeth will be the song
we step to, because they will not
be our teeth. Do you understand?
What I mean here is the last leg,
the foot in the grave, the last inches
of rope. They laugh, now. But
they mock their own demise, and so
we laugh, too.

God Bless america

God bless america,   this bitter and slender-necked stepsister
land that I love;   that I fear will kill me in my sleep or lynch me as I
stand beside her and   braid the blonde ropes of her hair, will not let me
guide her   'cross the canyon she has stretched between us. All
through the night   my screams float above her cup like steam. I, the darker sister
with a light   too dim behind the eyes, still smile with teeth dangling like stars
from above—   while her heel is thrust in my face. My bone's break is heard
from the mountains   in Georgia and
to the prairies   in Texas. She feeds me limb-by-limb
to the oceans,   back to the wet mouth of the Atlantic
white with foam   despite the spilt blood below. Sinking 'til sunk, I pray
God bless   my re-membered body, be made whole in one name, like
america,   the sister who denied me and kept her beauty. This
my   fickle family of bruise-blooded brothers I will call no
home sweet home   relative, no sibling, no flesh of mine.

To remember, Now

A noise above us always
now. We sleep. Eat. Go
to museums. Our daughters
laugh, not loudly enough.
The noise just above us still.
Mailboxes full of our names.
Something reaches for a knife.
Silence. But gone are we, down
a wary interstate. Above us,
the noise insists. Ghosts in
the rearview. A muted siren. And
we laugh. Cry, too. Fear doesn't
die, it changes—water to steam,
fire to smoke. Today is only water
to the left of us. Fire, on the right.
Waiting. A shoe in one hand.
We don't look over our shoulders.
We look up.

Uhmarekin History Suite

Look

Figure 1. All white kitchen. Bright light comes in from right side. A cabinet is opened.

This Way Comes

Figure 2. Woman stands
in the foreground
Wears khaki
shorts, a sleeveless
sweater. Sunglasses.
She is smiling.
Small flame burns along
siding of a house
several yards
behind her.

Fore

Figure 3. Close up. Woman's eye (left, brown). Eyebrow hair. The eye looks upward. Each hair has small, needlelike thorns along each strand. Background, a bathroom mirror revealing wad of bloody tissue, box of Band-Aids.

There

Figure 4. Foreground, a woman, a wolf stand in a clearing. Backs turned. They face the background and stare into night. Nothing ~~is there~~ is visible.

New Nature

Figure 5. Couple poses in front of stucco house. Pink. Stands next to "Sold" sign. Lemon tree to the left. Right, stucco wall. Palm tree rises behind house. A woman is carried, held by single palm leaf.

Wait in the Water

Figure 6. Man in bathtub. Eyes, nose, chin, and feet are seen. All other parts invisible when submerged in water.

Sasha's Waltz on the Wreckage

My eyes flicker at the brilliance
of my daughter's knife, the one
she has sharpened in each
of her lifetimes. It lays still, now,
as she dances before me in the
sun's eye. The rubble shifts below
her heel and there is the tooth of
some tired terror. It glints. Or smirks.

What joy is this that never knew us?
No fist looks to humble her beauty.
Nothing barrels between her
and her flesh. She is finally mine.
"Thass my song!" her hand reaches
for me, and I dance with my daughter.
I dance with my perfect daughter. I
hold her to me in love, instead of fear—
or want to.

Aunt Jemima

& Mammy subathing on the white house lawn

sunbathing on the white house lawn

Acknowledgments

The Mothers
Thank you to Bonita Banks, who is my most precious thing.
Thank you to Natasha Carrizosa who only ever wanted me to wear my own face.
Thank you to Giselle Robinson who I loved then and love now.
Thank you to Flora Mills who protected me when she barely knew me.
Thank you to Mendi Obadike, my Black Art Mom from whom I've only felt love.

& Sisters
Thank you Sophia Lynn & Sade LaNay
Thank you Ariana Brown & Jacqui Germain
Thank you Adriana Green & Maria Baker
Thank you Janae Williams & Bri Galbreath
Thank you Lyric Hunter & Ana Reyes-Bonar
Thank you Candice Iloh & Monét Marshall
Thank you Jill Louise Busby & Fajr Muhammad
Thank you Alisha Acquaye & Adjua Greaves

& Fathers
Thank you to Greg Banks, who I hope is made proud.
Thank you to John Stephenson, who I love and love and love.

& Brothers
Thank you Shannon Banks & Donney Rose
Thank you Michael Hatcher & Terry Otis
Thank you Chris Key & Dwayne Madden
Thank you Brother Jive & Jason Reynolds
Thank you Chad Mills

Particular thanks to Christian Hawkey, James Hannaham, Samantha Hunt, Pratt MFA, Marble House Project, Dianne Stephenson, and my Rhode Island Writers Colony family. I love you.

The following pieces from this work have appeared in the following publications:
- Sasha Fells the Wildwood—*BODY Literature*
- God Bless america—*PBS Newshour*
- If I Say I Hate My Country—*RHINO*
- Portrait of My Sister's Ankle Tied in Ribbon; america, MINE—*The Collagist*
- Upon Visiting Harriet Tubman's Grave—*Obsidian: Literature & Arts in the African Diaspora*
- Capitol Suite—*The FANZINE*
- Uhmareka, Pre Collapse; Uhmareka, Collapse; Uhmareka, Post Collapse; Uhmareka Post Post Collapse; Untitled (But Still a Warning Though)—*Poor Claudia*
- From Canfield Green...—*Apogee*